How to Get a Leasing Consultant Job!

It's Easy, Fun & You Don't Need a Degree!

By

Mary Bass

Table of Contents

1. **Introduction:**   3
2. **Qualities:**   6
3. **Cover Letter & Resume:** 9
4. **Looking for a Job:**   19
5. **Interviewing:**   25
6. **You've Got the Job!!:** 29
7. **Career:**   36
8. **Summary:**   38

Copyright 2018

INTRODUCTION

> "If you can dream it, you can do it."
>
> – Walt Disney

This book is intended to provide a good understanding of the job whether you have leasing experience or not. It's a great opportunity for students, internationals, people who like to work with people and those looking for a career transition, full or part-time.

I was inspired to write this book after being in property management for over 15 years, including running a small staffing agency, in which I saw tons of resumes and conducted tons of interviews. I worked on site for 10 years and then worked from home for a national vendor.

These are the things I learned that have worked for me and many others experiencing a successful career in property management. The best thing about this career is that it can be successful in so many ways and it all up to you and your career goals!

There are few jobs in which you can learn so much about real estate, selling and managing properties AND in which you can start a great career so easily! In fact, us oldies joke about how we just "fell into the industry" because we'd never heard of it until someone suggested it to us or ended up in a situation that presented the opportunity to us.

I started in the business when I moved to Miami from San Francisco to share an apartment with a friend that had moved there a few months before I got there. I was discouraged about my job prospects because Miami's transit system wasn't that great, and I didn't have a car. One day I went to the leasing office to fax off some resumes in my jammies and robe (I don't recommend this).

As I walked across the parking lot, I thought: "I just want a job in a career that I can have for the rest of my life – one that I love to do". At that moment, a flock of green canaries, quietly resting in a large leafy tree in the middle of the parking lot were startled by my presence and quickly flew up and away – it literally looked like the leaves had come alive and flew away all at once! Beautiful!

That lifted my spirits a little by the time I made it to the office. As I was faxing my resumes, the Leasing Agent and Property Manager were discussing how they needed another person and quick. I turned around and told them that I was looking for a job and handed them my resume. The manager took one look at it, then at me and told me I was hired. And so my career in property management began!

Up until now this was not a career option most people knew about, at least not here in the Seattle area. Then something happened – Seattle started growing exponentially! People from all over the world were suddenly looking for a place to rent because they got a job at Microsoft, Amazon or Google. Thus, creating the demand for apartments and fueling construction to build more to meet demand.

Seattle is one of the fastest growing cities in the country as of this writing. According to the Seattle Times, (March 16, 2018) more than 64k people moved to Seattle in 2017 - about 5k people a month and almost half were from another country. But you can get a leasing job anywhere in the U.S. where there are apartments!

According to the National Apartment Leasing Professional (NALP), current Leasing Agent salaries range from $13-$19 an hour nationally, $15 to $18 an hour in Seattle. Median income for a Leasing Manager, a relatively new position, is $45k. Nationally: $36,780 to $48,989. This includes commissions which are based on newly rented units and lease renewals. Commissions typically range from $20 to $100 each. Extra money is always good!

In Seattle, Assistant Managers start at about $20 per hour and Property Manager positions typically are paid depending on the number of units being managed – roughly $30 to $40 per unit, per month. These rates can vary nationally. Some management companies also pay managers based on net operating income (how well expenses compare to the income of the property or profit) and other financial factors.

This ebook will teach you what qualities hiring managers want in a candidate and how you can translate that onto your resume and cover letter so that gets you an interview and of course, the job!

You'll learn how to use different websites that will give you some insight into the company and where to find listings. Interview techniques and advice will be revealed as well as what your options are career-wise.

I'm also available if you have questions or need help with your resume. I welcome your feedback about this ebook. After owning and operating a staffing agency for 2 years, I'm restructuring my company. If you send me you email address, I'll send you the link when the new website is done: office@mystaffpmseattle.com.

This information is intended to help you, in an easy quick way, get the job that ignites your career! Now, let's get to it!

Disclaimer

Everything written in this material is based on my experience as an employee for 15+ years in residential property management in the Seattle area (only my first year in Miami, Fl.) working at various companies. Current statistical information offered is a result of researching many sources and are noted, when appropriate.

The material doesn't, in any way, represent any one company but rather a collection of methods and practices I've learned throughout my career.

It is in no way the last word about this dynamic ever-changing industry that will continue to evolve as Seattle does, creating more opportunities, due to the myriad of people moving to this area.

QUALITIES

"If you want a quality, act as if you already have it."
– William James

Innate

The main duties of a Leasing Consultant are keeping and maintaining high occupancy for the property. This is done by leasing available units, handling renewals and receiving current resident requests resulting in a overall good experience for residents and prospects. It's an entry-level position that can provide training for the Leasing Manager or Assistant Manager positions.

Innate qualities are ones that can't be taught – they are a part of a person's personality that's expressed naturally. There are a lot of great qualities that you'll find in any successful Leasing Agent (and Manager but more about that in my next ebook). They include these qualities:

- outgoing,
- friendly,
- self-motivated,
- the ability/willingness to work independently and as part of a team,
- genuine interest in people,
- upbeat attitude
- great listening skills.

A huge part of being a successful Leasing Agent is easy if you really enjoy meeting new people and helping them to select their next home. This is a big decision for anybody in any situation with many things to consider, the size, distance from work, comfort level, price etc., that normally takes a lot of research and work. Which is where you come in! You're there to provide solutions for this problem, or question.

This is true even if they don't choose your property. People like to purchase from people that they like. And they will always remember the great experience they had with you! I've had residents who came to tour with me, rented elsewhere and then ended up coming back to rent, sometimes up to a year later, because they liked the way I treated them. Being nice and truly wanting the best for your prospects goes a long way and it will make you more money.

Your guests can feel this sincerity and it's the best way to connect with them. Good listening skills are very important too. Really make sure that you understand what your visitors are looking for and write it down as they tell you so that your mind is focused on them and not your thoughts. And then repeat it back to them so that they know that you understand what they're saying. For example, "Great, so you're looking for a two bedroom, two bath that doesn't share a wall. I can help you with that – we have several units with that layout type that are available for when you want to move!" All with a smile, of course!

The great news is if you are a people person, then you're already half way there! This means you're a natural problem-solver.

And it's fun! Not to appear sexist but one of the reasons why I think that women tend to do well in property management is because we love everything about home. I know I never tire of talking about décor or what I love the most about the home or property that I'm working and living on. Home is where people live and is one of the most important topics you can discuss with anyone.

And it's the one thing that people will always want to talk to someone about before committing to rent or buy. I think that means that robots will never replace a real live Leasing Consultant!

Being self-motivated means that you don't need anyone to tell you to do your job and when it needs to be done. Once you know what to do, when you come in to work, on time, you just start doing it. Managers love to work with employees who do this! I've found that very few managers like to micro-manage. Probably because they can't – there's too much to do (reports, meetings etc.) and who wants to keep telling someone to do the something repeatedly anyways?

Possessing an upbeat attitude means you're a positive person in general. Not that you don't see reality, but you also see the opportunities or solutions and what could be reality too. And you're probably good at verbally painting that picture for others to see too. You're not a complainer and you tend to see the bright side more often. No one likes to work with a downer and being one won't lead you to success (anywhere) either.

The ability to drop personal conflicts at the door and not involve them in your work is preferred in any office. Sure, we all have lives in which things happen that have nothing to do with work but talking about them to prospects and your colleagues is inappropriate unless it's positive and you're truly friends with them.

In general, keeping the conversation to the question at hand, renting apartments and focusing on your residents and prospects is the best thing to do and part of being professional. I recommend positive chit chat with new colleagues until you get to know them better or just keeping it that way permanently.

Qualities That Can Be Learned

Qualities that can be taught include being professional, computer literate and organized as well as having sharp sales (including follow up) skills. The ability to do fourth grade math and having great communication skills are required too.

Being professional means that you are dressed appropriately, which is usually business casual (no open-toed shoes for safety reasons and no jeans or sneakers), having a friendly demeanor and greeting everyone with a smile even if there is a conflict.

In the training provided by your new company, you'll be given details as to how they would like you to do this specifically including how to prepare a lease and fully "move in" someone in the system. What is provided in this ebook is a general outline of what is normally done by most property management companies in the Seattle area. However, the process of leasing apartments is generally the same all throughout the country.

If you know how to work a smartphone, then you'll be fine learning the systems that track residents and prospects like Yardi or Appfolio and others that handle the application and lease signing processes. In addition, there's Word, Excel and email -all very easy to learn and use.

This also goes for the math part. Another feature of the systems you use will prorate rent and other fees for you when putting together a lease. Just be sure to quote the correct rates and fees to your prospects and applicants.

Good presentation skills include speaking clearly, using as little slang as possible while looking professional in business casual attire as well as presenting the property in such a way that it's a viable option for the prospect (according to what they're looking for in their new home). In training, you'll learn why most people want to rent at your property (features and benefits) and will be able to do this with practice, flawlessly, soon. You'll also want to read the property's website.

The system used to track guests will do a lot of the organizing for you. Just be sure to enter tour and work order information into the system before the end of the day. In this role, you typically won't be responsible for reports and paying invoices, so you won't have to worry about that but you will be expected to note every tour you've given each day and work orders.

Also, keeping your work space organized and clutter free looks better to prospects when they walk into the office – you don't appear too busy to stop what you're doing to give them a tour.

COVER LETTER & RESUME

> *"Big jobs usually go to people who prove their ability to outgrow small ones."*
> *- Ralph Waldo Emerson*

Before we get into the mechanics of your ideal resume and cover letter, let's look at the typical Leasing Consultant job description:

Reporting to the Property Manager, the Leasing Agent is the community's sales representative whose primary duties are to greet clients, to professionally present the features and benefits of the community and properly secure lease agreements from qualified persons that adhere to Fair Housing guidelines (you'll be trained on this too). This is a service focused position that strives to make current residents feel comfortable in their community so that they renew their leases as well as lease available units to new residents.

DUTIES AND RESPONSIBILITES

- Conduct all business in accordance with company policies and procedures, Fair Housing, Americans with Disabilities Act, Fair Credit Reporting Act, and all other Federal and State laws.
- Record all prospective resident visits in Yardi whether in person or by phone.
- Greet prospective residents and qualify their needs and preferences while professionally presenting the features and benefits of the community and specific apartments.
- Have prospects complete an application and secure deposit in accordance with company procedures and Fair Housing requirements. Correctly complete all lease applications, assist with application verification and notify prospective residents of results.
- Completes all lease paperwork including related addenda and handles rent collection.
- Update the availability report, process applications for approvals. (i.e., credit check, rental history, etc.). Submit processed applications to the Community Manager for approval. Follow up with applicant regarding status.
- Coordinate with maintenance to ensure apartment is ready for resident to move in on agreed date.

- Follow-up on prospects that did not rent and attempt to close the sale again. If unable to do so, refer them to sister or nearby communities that meet the prospect's needs.
- Secure the new resident's signature(s) on appropriate paperwork prior to move-in and make sure the resident physical and online files is complete with all required documents. Orient new residents to the community.
- Assist in monitoring lease renewals. Distribute and follow-up on renewal notices.
- Monitor advertising effectiveness by completing a monthly market survey report and shop competitive communities.
- Distribute all community-issued notices.
- Respond to resident requests, concerns, comments and communicate them to the Property Manager while consistently implementing community policies.
- Enter Maintenance Requests into the system at the time received.
- Ensure all maintenance repairs are handled satisfactorily by contacting residents to follow up on completed Service Requests on a weekly basis.
- Makes sure the office is always clean and clutter-free.
- Assist in planning resident functions. Attend functions and participate as host, as directed by the Property Manager.
- Participate in outreach marketing activities daily to obtain prospective residents by posting ads on Craigslist and updating online advertising to reflect current market pricing as needed.
- Make sure A board has fresh balloons each day.
- Willingness to obtain Fair Housing Certification.
- Demonstrate strong oral and written communication skills.
- Operate telephone, computer/keyboard, Microsoft Office including Word and MS Outlook and community software
- Must possess a positive attitude and smile under all circumstances.
- Participate in training to comply with new or existing laws.
- Ability to work a flexible schedule, including weekends.
- One year of experience in previous relevant customer service.
- Neat, clean, professional dress and demeanor whenever present at the community. Represent the company in a professional manner at all the times.
- Comply with expectations as demonstrated in the employee handbook.
- Successfully pass drug test and background check.
- Learn and ensure compliance with all company, local, state and federal safety rules. Ensures that unsafe conditions are corrected in a timely manner.
- Monitor office supplies monthly and report needs to property manager.

- Assists Property Manager and Assistant Manager in preparation of weekly reports, resident communications, etc.
- Performs any additional duties assigned by Assistant Manager, Property Manager or Regional Property Manager.

REQUIREMENTS

Excellent leasing and closing skills; good organizational and basic computer skills,

Work Hours: full-time, 40 hours/week, including weekends. Office hours are 9am to 6pm daily. Off days are Tuesday and Wednesday.

There is an occasional need to utilize personal transportation to visit competing communities and the corporate office.

Must be able to operate property golf cart to show homes to potential customers.

Must have valid driver's license and current automobile insurance.

Salary: $15- $19/hour plus commission, dependent on experience

Always read through to the bottom of the job description to make sure that you are qualified for the job, especially the Requirements section. If there is anything that may seem iffy, address it in your cover letter or don't respond to the ad. No need to waste time sending your resume to jobs that require previous leasing experience if you don't have any.

Cover Letter

It's a good habit to send a cover letter along with your resume. I know it can seem tedious, especially if you're responding to a lot of jobs ads but it's worth it. It makes you stand out since many people don't include one. The true purpose of a cover letter is to give the reader a chance to get to know you better.

Here's a cover letter checklist:
- ✓ Which position you're applying for, why and where you saw it listed.
- ✓ What you can contribute to the position and the property.
- ✓ Other ways your experience, qualities and skills can be applied to the position (this is where you refer to the Leasing Consultant job description responsibilities and requirements).
- ✓ That you're looking forward to hearing from them.
- ✓ Any specific questions the job description may call for you to answer.
- ✓ Save each tailored cover letter, labeling it in a way that's easy for you to find quickly on your computer. (By company is a convenient).

- ✓ When you are available for an interview
- ✓ Any job-related achievements you have

Your cover letter doesn't need to be long – just eager, positive and complete. The following is a sample Leasing Agent (or you'll see Leasing Consultant, it's the same position) job description and then an example of a cover letter tailored to it. The description was created by looking at multiple job descriptions to include everything you might see when looking for open positions.

When applying for jobs on websites like Indeed.com etc. you don't need to include the date – only the salutation and the body of the letter. If it's an attachment, then you want to include the date, the name and address of the company or property to which you are applying, the same way you would in writing a snail mail letter.

I used Craigslist below (you want to state whichever website you saw the listing). Also, be sure to include any information the employer asked for in the job description. Many times, this is requested to see how well you pay attention to details.

Sample Cover Letter (experienced):

(Today's Date)

Hiring Manager Name
Company Name
Company address

Dear (Hiring Manager or Name):

I'm applying for the Leasing Agent position that was listed on Craigslist. I feel that I'm qualified for this position due to my previous experience as a Leasing Agent and additional experience as a Sales Associate at a retail store. Attached is my resume.

I served as a Sales Associate in at Forever 21 and learned quite a bit – especially how to deal with people from a variety of backgrounds. I also learned how to sell products by listening to what my clients said they wanted and providing them with clothes that best matched their description by applying my product knowledge. In doing so, I earned the Best Sales Associate of the Year for the store!

Shortly afterwards, I became interested in working in a professional office environment. Now after a year as a Leasing Agent, I'm ready to apply what I have learned in this position in a company such as yours that has many opportunities for growth into a managerial position.

In my current position as Leasing Agent, I perform all the duties listed in the job description. In addition, I author the weekly reports for my Manager to review before it's sent to the corporate office and the owner.

I am available for an interview during my lunch breaks and my off day, Monday. Please feel free to contact me any time.

I look forward to hearing from you!

Thank you,

(your first and last name)
(phone)

Sample Cover Letter (inexperienced):

(Today's Date)

Hiring Manager Name
Company Name
Company address

Dear (Hiring Manager or Name):

I'm applying for the Leasing Agent position that was listed on Craigslist. I feel that I'm qualified for this position due to my volunteer experience in high school. I was the Marketing Manager for 2 years for the fundraiser committee for my class. I was responsible for raising funds to go on our class trip and fund other events.

I worked 10 hours a week on average, during the summer time too, marketing our cause to the surrounding community, individuals and businesses. Marketing efforts included cold calling, impromptu presentations and mailings. I personally raised $10k in a year.

While doing this I also maintained a 3.5 grade average and participated in sports and learned how to play the violin.

I think that this experience makes me highly qualified for this position. I'm excited to begin my new career in property management and would love to apply my skills and abilities to this dynamic position as an employee at (company name).

Please feel free to contact me at your convenience. I'm available any time for an interview.

I look forward to hearing from you!

Thank you,

(your first and last name)
(phone)

Your Resume

It's a representation of you on paper and it means a lot. If you sent a resume out to several companies and don't receive a call for an interview, then you need to change your resume and your cover letter.

There are a lot of different formats and basically Hiring Managers (HMs) want to get a good idea of your experience at a glance. The biggest reason why they may even look at it in the first place is because it contains certain keywords that their system uses to direct resumes to them (not all are). Good flag words: lease and sell - even if you don't have direct experience, find a way to use them on your resume.

When you write your resume, these are the things that should be checked off before it goes anywhere.

- All words are spelled correctly (make sure spellcheck and grammar check are turned on in your Word program and use an app similar Grammarly).
- You list the correct phone number where you want HMs to contact you.
- You don't have to put your address on it but if you don't, include at least the town and state (some job descriptions are circulated in several areas of the country).
- Generally, it should be no longer than 2 pages. Although that's not a strict rule (especially for those with 10+ years of relevant, valuable managerial experience)
- Each job entry should have the name of the company, position title, when you worked there, city and state of where you worked for them and 2-3 bullet points that describe, briefly, what you did for them.
- There should always be a section for Skills and Education and they should be accurate. You can leave off the year(s) you graduated college or high school if you have 10 years or more of experience. It's illegal for employers to ask you your age. List your college or high school but not both.
- Bullet points of your previous job experience should demonstrate how you contributed to the organization in a meaningful way in addition to the actual job duties performed. Choose words that are action and result oriented, verbs preferably and make sure you're using the correct tense (for example, "performed" versus "perform" is equal to a past job versus your current job. Sales achievements weigh in heavily. Try to keep them as brief as possible.
- Tailor your resume to the job description. Like properties, not all positions, are the same.
- Always send a cover letter. This is how the HMs gets to know you outside of your resume. More details about those components follow.

- ❖ Including an objective is also good, especially if you don't have a lot of work experience. It should tie in with the job you're responding to and not be too general. For example: "To get a job in an office" doesn't sound as good as "To gain administrative experience working in a law firm." Not including one is okay too.
- ❖ Any gaps in time should be explained briefly and clearly, on your resume and cover letter.
- ❖ Read it aloud carefully a couple times before sending it out, you will catch most, if not all, mistakes.

These points may seem elementary, but you would be surprised at the resumes I've gotten (and other HMs) that didn't adhere to the above guidelines, especially when a lot of this information is readily available on the internet.

Refer to the following sample resume. You'll see many other formats on the internet but this one is most often used. It really doesn't matter how it's formatted, so long as it's easy to read and doesn't require HMs to search for the information they.

The following is a sample resume template:

First & Last Name
City, State, Zip Code
email address
phone number

Objective: To become a successful Leasing Consultant and grow into an Assistant Manager position within a great property management company!

EXPERIENCE

(Company Name); (City, State)
Leasing Consultant, 96 units   2/16 - present

- Brought occupancy from 81% to 100% within 3 months by utilizing online marketing tools to advertise units and experienced leasing skills
- Service resident requests, via phone and in person, that include work orders, rent collection, general questions etc.
- Won the company's Best Leasing Consultant Award 2017

(Company Name); (City, State)
Sales Associate   1/14 - 1/17

- Kept selling floor tidy
- Serviced customers by answering questions, checking stock in the storeroom, replacing clothes onto the sales floor from the dressing rooms etc.
- Sales were higher by 4% during my shifts

(Company Name); (City, State)
Customer Service Agent   10/12 -12/13

- Serviced up to 50 customers per day with very detailed orders, initiated them as well as adding details to current orders
- Worked quickly and accurately while delivering a good experience for the customer

Skills: Yardi, Microsoft Word, Customer Database, Microsoft Suite, Excellent Customer Service, Sales

Education: (school name and degree – specialization and year graduated or attended)
Read ebook: How to Get a Leasing Consultant Job!

This is a traditional resume that is tried and true. I've only used this format and it's gotten me a lot of interviews and a lot of jobs over the years. You can find it doing a search on the internet or creating your own in Word. Go with your gut and format your resume in a way that you think best reflects the real you and that will get you the interview.

If you need help with your resume, send me an email at office@mystaffpmseattle.com and you'll get details about how to get your resume in tip top shape.

There are some more do's and don'ts when it comes to resumes:

Don't:

- List adjectives in its own section to fill up space – it just screams "I'm not professional and/or I'm a beginner". There's nothing wrong with being inexperienced, it's just a matter of taking the experience you do have and applying it to the position you want in a professional, creative way.
- Make up your job title or duties or lie about them. It always catches up with you, even if you have references that will say you did them. And especially if they're duties that you will be responsible for in your new job.

Do:

- Make sure that it's easy to read and flows in sequence of time no matter what format you use. Employers will want to know how long you were at each of your previous positions.
- Include a cover letter. Not having one is like filling out half of a job application. It's not a good look.
- Mention any education material that you think helped you a lot in your jobs. Hopefully this book is one of them and you are welcome to put it on your resume and in your cover letter.

Hiring for a position can be very tedious. It requires a lot of time and effort, so it can be disappointing for the employer and the employee if it doesn't work out. For this reason and others, employers may use assessment tools and sometimes a long hiring process just to make sure that the person applying really wants the position. This process really weeds out the ones that don't and/or who are not qualified.

Keep in mind, if you are living in an area like Seattle where there are plenty of jobs and less than 1% unemployment, you are competing against a lot of people. It's wise to apply only for positions that you really want versus as many as possible to see who calls you back. The more focused you are in your job search, the better chance you have of getting the one that you want quicker.

LOOKING FOR A JOB

"The best way to predict the future is to create it."

- Abraham Lincoln

Once your resume looks razor sharp and you have a cover letter that'll knock any Hiring Manager's socks off, you're ready to start looking for your next great job!

This will all depend on whether your main goal is to just get a job any where or if you're looking for a career.

If you're just looking for a job, then it will be easier because all residential property management employers are always looking for Leasing Agents. Mainly due to high turnover. This is also the employee pool that gets fished from when HMs are looking for someone to promote into an Assistant or Property Manager. If you stay and do well in a leasing position for a year or longer, then HMs assume that you like the business and you will be promoted.

The other reason for a high turnover in this position is that some people find out that the position isn't right for them. And that's ok because the employee and the employer didn't invest too much effort before finding this out and it's expected that not every single person will love the job. It's not for everyone and it's worth it to find the right person for the job. No employer wants you to remain in a position that you don't like and it will affect your commissions. Bottom line: happy people sell more.

In areas like Seattle, there are always lots of ads for Leasing Agents because new apartments are being built every day. Other slower growth areas may not be as hot, but these positions are generally easier to find and tend to be available more often than managerial ones.

Job Websites

There are several great websites to you can use to search for jobs. The ones I like best are: Indeed, SimplyHired and good old Craigslist. It seems to me that every company will advertise with one of these sites. I really like SimplyHired and Indeed because they tell you how much the position pays. For the inexperienced that may not matter as much as experienced candidates who really want to know what years of direct experience is worth to a potential employer.

When you see a listing, the first thing you want to do is check out the company with Glassdoor. There may be reviews from angry employees that you may not consider but if there 20 or more, this will give you a idea of what it's like to work there or at least what those employees liked about their experience. Try to find reviews that are from your area and for the same position.

You'll see ads on Craigslist that don't have a company listed. Typically, it's either a recruiter, or the company itself, who for some reason want to remain confidential – usually small, local companies. As I gained more experience, I didn't respond to these ads, especially if I was already working and didn't want my current employer to know I was looking. But if you don't have a job or if you're current employer knows you're looking, then it's ok to answer them.

Living on the Property

One of the best things about this business is the ability to live on site for a discounted price! Typically, the discount is 20% for employees but may vary all the way to having a free apartment or lower (usually offered to managers). Most companies do offer a percentage off though.

You want to make sure that you can still afford the apartment by knowing what your take home pay will be (after taxes) once your rent is taken out. And there is usually a limit to how many people can live on site for each property. Your Manager can give you further details.

As of now, there is a tax advantage of having your rent taken out of your salary before you get it – it's not taxed so you fall into a lower tax bracket, so you end up paying less in taxes. However, I am in no way a tax advisor so please check with your tax preparer before moving on site.

We all know how beautiful life is without a commute! You save so much money and energy when you can walk to work, eat lunches at home and enjoy the amenities that you're selling.

The only disadvantage I found was that sometimes residents will think it's okay to come to your apartment door. I found that I didn't have this problem when I was working at better properties (A or B). Otherwise, the best way to deal with this is to politely tell residents that your off work and that if they need something, they need to go to the office.

One time when this happened: I asked him how he would feel if his customers suddenly knocked on his apartment door? A sales associate himself, he quickly apologized and went to the leasing office.

Property Management Categories

Conventional

Conventional properties that are not subsidized by the federal or local government. Although they can accept prospective residents who receive government benefits AND meet all application criteria. Their monetary benefits are counted as income.

Each category will attract its own type of demographic (household type) to it depending on where it's located, what amenities it offers as well as quality and price of the units.

If you're just starting out and have the opportunity, I recommend trying out more than one category of properties so that you can get an idea of what type of properties you like to work and live on.

You and the maintenance staff will make sure the amenities stay in good working order. The less amenities there are, the less involvement you have with residents making it even more important to have events or other types of resident services to foster resident retention.

Affordable/HUD Housing

HUD or affordable housing is government subsidized. These properties are required to be compliant with affordable housing guidelines and must submit paperwork to government agencies to rent to low income households (who may not otherwise afford to live there).

All information in this ebook is focused on conventional housing, as that is my experience. However, you will never be out of a job if you choose this category because it's so specialized. It has its own challenges and tends to pay a little less than conventional residential housing. Many employees I've met working at these properties also have a special interest in working with this demographic.

Other Types of Residential Housing

    Microunits

These are mini apartments, typically less than 350 square feet, that are popular in Seattle now and are usually less than 100 units per building. They usually hire a Resident Manager to live on site to monitor common areas and sometimes complete maintenance requests. Salaries usually can consist of a free deeply discounted apartment.

Older/Small Buildings

Usually less than 100 units, these properties also hire Resident Managers in the same capacity and have a similar salary structure.

Student Housing

As the name says, these are apartments that are dedicated to colleges and universities and can be mainly staffed by students.

50+ Housing

Demand for housing for 50+ has skyrocketed due to the healthier baby boomers and previous generations, who retire in another state but keep an apartment in the area because of family. This is different from assisted living homes as the apartments are conventional and are not equipped with any medical facilities. This is another new prosperous option of the housing market.

Property Classifications

The letters below refer to classifications of properties, no matter what category they fall into (although it's hard to find a class A property that would be considered a HUD property).

A: These are luxury properties that have lots of amenities like a pool, sauna, package delivery, concierge, etc. and generally have the highest rents in their surrounding market. They can be new construction or newly renovated. Units are of a higher quality with better appliances and residents are generally higher than average income households.

B: These properties may have some amenities. Rents and unit quality are average attract a demographic that represents middle America with average incomes.

C: The biggest difference with properties in this category is maintenance of the units and overall property appearance (a.k.a "curb appeal"). Units typically reflect the same lower than standard attention to detail with lower grade appliances, carpet etc.

D: Generally, the demographic that are attracted C and D properties are those with problems that hinder their acceptance to And B properties that involve problems with income, credit score, criminal background or rental history.

Having worked at all types of properties, I've observed that none of them are not without their challenges, they're just different within each category.

If it's important to you that you want to work, and possibly live, at a certain type of property, then be sure to at least look at the company's website and their ads on Craigslist (or another site that advertises apartment rentals) to see what type of property it is. Visiting the property is best. When looking to live on a property, you'll want to see what it looks like on a weekend night as well.

Asking Leasing Agents about their jobs when they're available is another great way to find out if you think you'd like working on that type of property and it's free! Just don't do it during the first five days of the month (rent collection time) and any other time that you see that the office is busy. But otherwise employees are likely to appreciate your questions.

Your intention is to target the right jobs for you by making sure you meet the job's qualifications/requirements and that fall in line with the type of work, and possibly living, environment you're looking for before applying for the position.

Staffing Agency

In my early days, I used staffing agencies often to get a job. They have established relationships with their clients so all you have to do is interview with them before being placed on assignment. Some of their clients will ask to interview you – usually if it's a direct hire placement.

If you are new to the field and/or don't know which type of property best suits you, I would recommend a staffing agency. This way you get more experience and get an idea of what type of property best suits you.

The pay will be a few dollars lower than if you were hired directly because the agency needs to take a cut. But that's very little to pay to get into a company you'll be happy with versus getting hired full time and then realizing that you don't like the work environment, location or something else meaningful to you. Assignments can be for as little as a day up to indefinitely.

It can sometimes be tough finding an agency that can place you right away. I suggest interviewing with at least 3 agencies. Unfortunately, agencies will encourage you to send your resume to them because they need a continuing flow of resumes coming into their office, whether they have jobs or not. Being flexible with pay will help you immensely. If you don't get an assignment after a week or so, then move on. They will call you if or when they have something. Your agency is as good as your recruiter.

As you're doing this, continue to apply to online job listings too. The more you do, the more chance you have of getting a job, especially if you have some leasing experience (at least 6 months, preferably a year or more).

Career Fairs

You'll see ads for Career Fairs hosted by very large property management companies like Greystar or staffing agencies. The Washington Multi-Family Housing Association (WMFHA) is also doing them now too. This is a great way to find a job too. You'll find more info about them on their websites.

INTERVIEWING

"There's never a second time to make a first impression."
— Will Rogers

So now that you've sent you're resume out to the leasing world, someone thinks you're a great fit for the position and they call you for an interview! Yaaay!

Usually there will be a phone interview first to determine if you will proceed to the next step, which is the face to face interview, but this may vary. At this point, management companies aren't using Skype to interview but I'm sure it will happen soon! Some companies will have you take online assessments before the interview.

Employers take great care when it comes to interviewing. No Hiring Manager wants to hire someone and then do it all over again in the next few months for the same position. And it may reflect on the Hiring Manager how well the new person fits into the position. For that reason, many managers will sometimes have you meet with the rest of the team. Based on their feedback, the manager can get an idea of how well you'll get along with them.

Here are some pointers:

- Most offices are business casual, so you don't have to wear a suit but feel free to do so. For woman, a nice blouse and skirt (professional length) or pants is fine. Men usually wear khakis and a polo or nice tee-shirt. Most companies have some attire that they give you (or you can buy) that has their name on it for you to wear at work. Any headwear worn for religious purposes are permitted.
- Bring a pad of paper to write notes. Even if you don't use it, it shows that you are interested in the details of the job and want to be sure to capture them, especially if you're given instructions.
- Know the answers to average interview questions including gaps in your resume etc. (Next are typical questions you're likely to be asked during the interview).
- Keep your answers to the point, professional and positive. No long drawn out "he said, she said" stories. What the interviewer wants to know is the answer to the questions and not to be taken on a long journey through the tedious details of a negative encounter.
- If you're unfamiliar with the location, arrive early to make sure you have time to find it, get a parking space or walk from public transit.

> Bring a copy of your resume and the job description with you in a folder or 8.5x11 envelope (not folded up inside your purse or pocket).
> Listening is key to making sure you understand what is being asked of you in the interview as well as when working. One technique that will help you is repeating the question before answering it. This will give your mind a chance to give you the answer, if you don't have one readily available.

Typical Interview Questions

There's been a lot written on this subject, so I just chose questions that relates most to working on an apartment community. I encourage you to memorize the answers to at least 10 questions and be able to answer them in a personable way (and you will after a few interviews). One of the main things the interviewer is looking for is how well you can connect over the phone. Email is the preferred way for many prospects to communicate now so you will be using it more often but there is still quite of bit of phone work involved in the position.

Why do you think you're a good fit for the job? If you're inexperienced (or none in property management), you want to highlight the duties of the job and how you have performed the same or similar tasks in another position or experience (volunteering for example). If you're right out of school, talk about those tasks in the context of the extracurricular activities you've participated in, part-time jobs or school projects. Your intention is to tie together what is required of the job and your experience to create a picture of you in the Leasing Agent position.

If you're experienced, this is easier. Keep track of your work achievements and mention them on your resume as well as in the interview.

Tell me a little about yourself? What the interviewer is really asking is for you to summarize your work experience as it relates to the position. So, you want to start with a position or something you liked doing at a previous work experience(s) and tie it in to why you chose to apply for a Leasing Consultant position, like it was the next logical choice

You're giving a short story about the person behind the resume – you. A nice thing I'm noticing here in Seattle is that employers aren't asking if you ever got fired from a job. If you have, don't bring it up unless they do. If so, tell a great story, briefly, and make it as positive as you can.

Tell me of a time when you handled a conflict (manager, customer or resident) and how was it resolved? Choose a work situation that highlights how you were able to resolve it in a positive manner. What happened and what were you thinking? What was your intended outcome in dealing with this situation? The Hiring Manager is trying to see how well you can make decisions in "the heat of the moment" and it's a good opportunity to show them how you shined in that situation. Was there a negative consequence that was avoided due to you being proactive? Even better - do tell!

You've got someone on the phone, a person at your desk and other people trying to get your attention – who takes priority? The answer is always the person in front of you. You may get this question even if you are experienced. You are being tested on your customer service skills. The reason why it's the right answer is because the person in front of you is more than likely either a resident or a prospect and how you treat them directly relates to the bottom line of the property's budget. No one wants to live at a property where they aren't treated well. So, that's why, even if your Regional or someone else from the corporate office, would understand you not making someone wait while you answer the phone. And will defend that decision to their owner client.

Vendors are employees that work for a company that supply products or services to the property - painters, cleaners, pest control, advertising sources etc. You would connect them with the employee they need to see <u>while</u> doing your tasks. In other words, it's fine to multitask. They understand and don't need to be entertained.

Why should we hire you versus other candidates that applied for the position? Your prospective employer is wanting to know what makes you stand out. They've seen hundreds of resumes and conducted a lot of interviews and who knows how many other people have applied for the position with similar or better experience. What makes you different? What you want to do is to choose a challenge that someone in that position will need to overcome or with the property and tell them how you have or will (or both) overcome it successfully. Highlighting your customer service and sales skills are always good ways to answer this question. You can also use an innate quality that you possess and expand on how it's perfect for the position since it can't be taught and not everyone has it.

What are your strengths? This one should directly reflect the requirements that are needed in the position. Describe at least 2.

What are your weaknesses? This is kind of a trick question because what you want to do is express it as a weakness but answer with something that employers like to hear. For example, you may work late to get things done for the next day because you want to start out fresh the next morning which means you're a perfectionist. Or proactive because you like to close out (follow ups and other office tasks) the day at the end of it instead of the next morning when it may be busy. If they ask you how this a weakness is, you can say that it puts a dent on your social life and then smile! Whichever one you choose, always explain it in a way that is truly a good thing to do.

What kind of work environment do you prefer? You would just point out the things you like about your prospective work place that you think you'd enjoy. Perhaps a previous job experience(s) if the job you're applying for has the same kind of work environment too.

What is the toughest decision you made recently or ever? What happened and why did you make that decision? Describing a work situation would the best way to answer this question. If you don't have any, you can use a personal one – just make sure it's brief and to the point. Clearly explain the circumstances or the problem and what decisions you made. Don't get overly emotional – try to remain positive and objective by pointing out the positive consequences of the situation.

Do you have any questions for me? Yes, always. Here are a few:

- What is the next step?
- When are you looking to have this position filled?
- What are the greatest challenges others find or have found with this position? This is a great opportunity to tell the interviewer how you would best overcome this challenge if you haven't already by the end of the meeting.
- Why did the previous person in this position leave?

Follow Up

You will always want to follow up every interview with an email thanking the interviewer for his/her time. It should be sent as soon as possible up until the end of the next business day. Your intention is to plant another seed in the interviewer's head about you. Mention something in the conversation such as why you think you're the best person for the job. It can be almost anything but should be memorable and positive.

If you haven't heard anything from them a couple of days after you've sent your thank you letter, it's okay to follow up again to see if they made their decision. However, most companies will send an email to candidates that were interviewed once the position is filled.

If you don't hear anything after the 2nd follow up, then you can assume you didn't get the job.

YOU'VE GOT THE JOB!!

"Looking for a job is like target practice: don't waste bullets (energy) on shooting in the air – carefully aim at your target."

- *Mary Bass*

But let's assume you do! You did an amazing job on the interview(s), passed the background and drug test and you are the chosen one – yaaaay! Congratulations! You're are now officially a Leasing Consultant!

Here is a quick rundown of the general process for a new move in – there are a lot of parts that can vary by applicant and company policy. You will be trained on this process and after doing it a few times you'll memorize the procedure. Getting a checklist of this process, or making your own, is extremely helpful.

New Move-In Process

1. Applicant **tours** a home with you.
2. Applicant puts a **hold** on an apartment by paying a fee (sometimes called an administrative fee) that is not refundable if they cancel the unit unless it's a courtesy hold (prospect can cancel within 48 hours and get their money back).
3. Applicant does the following (required):
   - Fill out an **application** (online probably)
   - A **criminal** background is done by a vendor company
   - Either you or the vendor company will call to get **rental references**.
   - Applicant must supply **proof of income** which is usually their most recent paystubs (2) or offer letter; income typically must be 2.5 to 3 times the amount of the monthly rent, before taxes (i.e. for a $2000/month home, the applicant needs to make at least $5000/month including taxes)
4. Applicant is **approved.** The process stops here if they're denied and you would inform them.
5. You tell the applicant their **total move in fee amount**. The lease should specify and breakdown this amount too.
6. **Move-In Day**:
   - Depending on your company policy, you would **go over the lease** or on their own. Many Seattle city properties have residents review and sign the lease online so that's already done by this time or they will do so at your office.

- You'll make a **copy of their current ID** (passport or driver's license) as well as print out their lease and other addenda for the physical files.
- Do an **inspection of the unit** with the resident. I would do mine ahead of time and let them know that I made sure everything was suitable. Then I'd just wait while they look around. Note any damage in the unit, not regular wear and tear, that the resident might be charged for and enter any necessary work orders for items that need to be fixed (there shouldn't be any).
- Both of you **sign the move in sheet** and you give a copy to the resident.
- Give the resident their **keys**.
- **Apply funds in system** as you change the status of the applicant to that of a resident in the system on the same day.
- Set up their **utilities** and place confirmations in the folder (some require that this is done on the same day).
- **Complete all other items** on the checklist for physical resident files.

7. **Follow up** 2 – 3 days later with the resident to see how everything is going and if they have any questions.

Your new company will train you in their policies and procedures but there are a few basic things that you should keep in mind:

- Take notes – not only are they good to refer back to but when you do this, it's like depositing the information into your memory bank. You are way more likely to remember something when you write it down. It also helps to organize and connect the information in your head in a cohesive way. And you can also use it as a checklist until it becomes a part of your routine.
- Speaking of, checklists are awesome! Most companies will have a task checklist for you to follow each day and one for each process as well (i.e. doing a move out). This way you don't forget anything and can work independently and sometimes quicker. Even after you've settled into the job, I recommend using checklists. Leasing offices can be very busy so having checklists ensures you get everything done, in a timely manner and prevents you from spending more time on one task than needed.
- In this age of texts, it's still important to spell words correctly and format your responses to prospective residents. The following is a typical inquiry from someone looking for an apartment and the right way to respond:

Email Inquiry:

Hello,

I'm looking for a 2-bedroom apartment to move in to next month. Can you please tell me your availability?

Thank you,

Susan

Your response (the information won't be the same, but it should be formatted this way):

Hi Susan,

Thank you for contacting us!

Yes, we do have 2 bedrooms available for the time you'd like to move. They range from $1850 to $2050.

When would you like to come in for a tour?

Thanks,

(your first name or email signature)

Always remember to thank the person for contacting your property. The main purpose of the email is to get them to come in for a tour, if they are looking to move at the time your units will be available to see. With a friendly tone, qualify them in as little words as possible and if you have what they are looking for then try to get them to make an appointment to tour the property.

Suggested tour times are a half hour after the office opens to a half hour before it closes. That way you you'll have a chance to open and close the office, so you can clock out on time. You can be flexible with morning times but always leave at least a half hour for yourself since you never know what else may pop up.

And if they don't happen to rent this time with you, they might the next time they're looking to move because you gave them such great customer service!˙ People always remember when they received great service – which leads us into our next topic.

Great Customer Service = Great Commissions!!

Customer service is the name of the game in property management. It's always appreciated, it sells and adds immeasurably to the bottom line of any organization and your pocket! It also is the difference between a "good" property and its opposite and in anything in between. When guests and residents feel they are being treated well, they think well of the property and the people that manage it.

That's a huge selling point for every lease and renewal. And it will guarantee you a steady stream of extra income! Prospective residents always remember people who truly try to help them. They'll appreciate you giving pertinent information that could help them in deciding where to live – whether they decide to move to your property or not. I've even had residents go elsewhere (usually for the price) and then come back to my property to rent because they realize that they made a mistake.

That's why being positive is a wonderful attribute to have because if you're that type of person, you're already being this way in your everyday life so it's easier it is for you to do it at work!

Your employer or manager may train you in techniques of how to deal with difficult and prospective residents in a way that is polite, firm (when needed) and that adhere to Fair Housing standards.

Here are a few ways you can maintain a high level of customer service:

- **Listening** is key to finding the best unit for your prospects. After listening and writing down (on paper or in the system) what they are looking for, my question is always: "What are the top one or two things you really need to have you next home?" Their answer will allow you to hone in on those units that would best suite their desires. Now there will be times that the units you have available don't have those characteristics and that's ok. Tell them that and offer to show the unit anyway. Most of the time they will want to see it and you never know. It's your desire to help them that is most important. That's what they will remember.
- **Offering drinks and a seat** is the norm when receiving a guest and should be each time before a tour. It really sets a nice unrushed tone to the visit. This also works when a resident comes to you with a question or concern. You should always offer residents a seat and something to drink (and a snack, if you have any). This is also true with upset residents too - it's hard to be angry or upset when one is seated.

- **Writing down requests,** whether they're guest cards for tours or from residents, is an important part of the job. No one expects you to remember everything, but your employer will expect you at least to write down what prospective residents are looking for and work orders. You will be given a pad or guest cards, or you can simply type the info into whichever system the company is using. It's best to be accurate, brief and answer any questions that might be asked of you by maintenance for work orders or your manager for tours. You'll get the hang of this after doing it a few times. I also found it convenient to have a blank pad to jot things on throughout the day. That way I could jot things down that could be done later and make sure to do them before I left for the day.
- **Follow up,** as previously mentioned, is always important. It really makes a difference with your commissions and keeping the property occupied. You should really get used to closing out your requests or items each day. Did you follow up with completed work orders to make sure it was fixed to the resident's satisfaction? Did you follow up with the tours you had the previous day to see if they had any questions (if the system doesn't automatically do that for you)? Did you get back to any residents with answers to their questions that had nothing to do with work orders? The quicker you get in the habit of doing this the quicker you'll be promoted and the more money you'll make from more renewals and new leases.
- **Honesty** is always the best policy no matter what and that includes when you've made a mistake. Mature adults own up to their mistakes and learn from them so that they aren't repeated. No need to make a big deal out of it though - we're all human.
- **Recommendations** - For tours who want a layout that you don't have, mention the units you do have and recommend your sister properties. Or one of the properties that are on your market survey.
- **Multi-tasking** - During tours and when residents are communicating to you, don't multitask, if possible. Let the phone ring. You can always listen to the voicemail and call them back later. If they don't leave one, they'll call back.
- **Appointments** – Always schedule your tours unless there's always someone in the office that can do a tour when you're not there. Use your calendar so you don't double book yourself. Even when you do, you may also have more than one tour group anyway – especially when you're working alone on a weekend.

    The one that had an appointment is the one that goes first. If they mention that it's ok to have the other group tag along, then that's ok but don't suggest it. When anyone goes through the trouble of making an appointment, they want to meet with you, as you would be when you're looking for an apartment. Of course, if there's another person that can

take the other tour, that would be optimal. Don't assume that your manager can take the other tour, but you can ask. Many times, there are reports and other things that he/she must deal with, unbeknownst to you.
- **Professional** - Be personable but not too casual. It's about them, not you. Ways to maintain this balance is to keep focused on their needs. On a tour, be sure to tell them all the features and benefits that you think they might like but be sure not to go into long detailed stories that are not focused on their needs. When a resident comes to you with a request or concern, make sure you understand what they are saying (repeat it back to them) before giving your answer. If you don't have the answer, be sure to get it at the time they ask, if possible. If not, follow up with them later the same or next day.

Work Orders

One of the most consistent requests you'll receive are work orders or maintenance requests.

- Type them directly into the appropriate system if possible (recommended even more so than writing it down since you might forget to enter it into the system):
- True emergencies are defined as fire, flood or blood. In these instances, you can call maintenance or the manager directly before putting them into the system for obvious reasons.
- The requests you'll get most of the time are for appliances and plumbing. You want to remember to always say exactly where the trouble is and be as specific as possible. For example, if there is a double sink, which one of the two is clogged? Or if the garbage disposal is making a humming noise when turned on, did you ask the resident if they pressed the reset button on the bottom of it before entering a work order? If that didn't work, mention it in the work order. You'll be trained on what other questions you should ask for a variety of other work orders too.
- You want to make sure that maintenance can find the right area to fix without having to come back and ask you or the resident a question. It just delays the process. The bigger the property, the bigger deal this is.
- Make it a habit to ask the resident if we have permission to enter the unit if they aren't there when maintenance arrives. It's illegal to enter a resident's apartment without their permission, so you must ask this question for each work order.

Market Surveys

Market Surveys, completed each month, are the main way you and your office team will know what the competition, or the market, is doing. The information contained in them will determine at which rate your rents will be set, how well your property is doing compared to nearby properties and a great way to get ideas for resident events!

Typically, the properties listed on the market survey will be those that your prospects will choose from in that neighborhood. The information it provides can include: occupancy and leased percentages, property contact information, rental rates for each type of unit, how many of each unit there is, and which positions are staffed at the property.

Another reason why Market Surveys are great is that they give you a chance to chat with your neighboring properties and form a good relationship with them. I've recommended properties that were on my market survey if I didn't have any sister properties in the neighborhood and they will do the same for you!

Make it a goal to visit them once a quarter or at least once a year. When you see what other properties your prospects are touring, you're better able to sell them on the benefits and features of your property.

Weekly Reports

Usually all reports besides the Market Survey are done by the Assistant Manager or Property Manager. However, when you're comfortable in your position and interested in being promoted, it's a good idea to get a jump on some reports that are required of in your next position. The Manager would be more than happy to get the extra help too!

Weekly reports are sent to the Regional Manager and/or the Owner of the property. It tells what activities transpired for the week including leases, what the units rented for, their market rents, units in the process of make ready (units being readied for the next resident), events, who gave notice etc.

It's an easy excel spreadsheet that has formulas that auto-populates certain fields when you change the information in the linked main fields.

CAREER

"Choose a job you love, and you will never have to work a day in your life."
- Confucius

There are quite a few career paths open to you in property management! I started out as a Leasing Consultant, then became an Assistant Manager at a large property (300+ units) before becoming a Manager for 3 small properties (up to 100 units each). Then because the I was so impressed by a vendor representative that came to my property one day that I decided to try doing that. I loved working from home, having my own schedule, working independently to meet company goals and of course, receiving larger commissions!

You're always good at doing what you love. So just find out what you love in property management, see which job requires most of what you love to do and then choose a job whose description matches that!

Maintenance is another option if you're good at fixing things. Being such a completely different position, we won't discuss it here but look out for future ebooks that will focus on maintenance.

Let's cover the following positions you'd typically see on job websites, so you'll get an idea of the career options you have to choose from:

- **Concierge** Similar a hotel, this job entails making sure that all visitors are greeted and taken care of in various ways that don't involve leasing apartments or rent collection. These positions are usually large properties located in metropolitan areas. It's a great position for someone new to the job market.
- **Leasing Consultant** Markets and leases available units. Responds to resident questions and concerns regarding their home. What this book is all about.
- **Leasing Manager**: Manages Leasing Consultants. Also, usually offered at larger properties this is a relatively new position. It's a good move from being a Leasing Consultant or Resident Manager.
- **Assistant Manager:** Does most or all the property's reporting: weekly, monthly and quarterly in addition to processing invoices and leasing when needed. One can expect to spend 6 months to about 2 years in this position before being promoted to a Property Manager.

- **Property Manager:** Responsible for everything that happens on the property including maintenance. The buck stops with him/her, so to speak. Many employees love this position and choose to stay in it for the rest of their career, working at various properties.
- **Resident Manager:** Usually required to live on site and perform maintenance requests. Properties are usually less than 100 units and managed by local companies.
- **Regional Manager or Asset Manager:** Linking the corporate office and owner to the properties, this position has a set amount of them that they oversee to ensure they're being managed according to company policy, profitability and the owners request.
- **Vendor:** Properties would be at a loss without their vendors – especially those that provide their most basic services such as the landscapers, cleaners and painters. At larger companies, especially national ones, a sales representative is hired to service a given territory of current client properties and tasked with bringing on more.
- **Entrepreneur:** A person who runs a small business. In this case, a product or service dedicated to residential property clients.

It's not surprising that many property management professionals start their own business since managing a property operates the same in many ways. The same entrepreneurial attitude that it takes to run a profitable community is the same one it takes to run a small business. Many people have made the decision to run their own business after years in property management, relying on the relationships they've made to support their new business.

No matter how you map your career, if you love it, you'll always do well!

SUMMARY

> *"It's not the days in your life,*
> *but the life in your days that counts."*
> *- Brian White*

I hope you've learned a lot about being a Leasing Consultant and that you feel more confident about pursuing this career path. I also encourage you to contact me with any questions or to get help with your resume at office@mystaffpmseattle.com.

Also, watch out for my future ebooks about other property management positions that will teach you what you need to know and do to snag one of them! Let me know if you want to be contacted when it becomes available.

And of course, if you feel this publication has helped you get a job, I want to know about that too!

This is truly a fascinating, fun, exciting industry that's bursting with opportunities. Just decide which career path you'd like to take and go for it, fearlessly!

I wish you the best of luck!

www.ingramcontent.com/pod-product-compliance
Lightning Source LLC
Chambersburg PA
CBHW031513210526
45464CB00007B/2888